E

Escape Your Prison's

A Path from Chains to Happiness

By: Jody Forehand

Escape Your Prisons

Copyright 2020

***ALL RIGHTS RESERVED：** No parts of this publication may be reproduced or transmitted in any form whatsoever, electronical, mechanical, photocopying, by any informational system, or retrieval system without the express written consent of the author.*

Dedication

This book is dedicated to all those who are standing behind prison walls and struggling to see freedom. You are worth more than you believe and after reading this, I hope that you will see your true worth!

Introduction

The word prison suggests, bars, chains, criminals, guards, walls. We tend to think of the physical side of incarceration where only the scourge of society, and lowly amongst us reside. There is also another type of prison where far more people are held captive by unmanned walls and mental, or emotional chains weighing them down. I have been in prison. I spent fourteen years and ten months in the Michigan Department of Corrections. My inmate number was 236247. I spent even longer in a mental and emotional one the lasted thirty-two years. I know a thing or two about being incarcerated. The chains that bound me in a mental and emotional prison were far more excruciating then any man-made shackles.

Self-hatred, low self-esteem, poor body image, feeling not good enough, these are all examples of prisons. A lot of us have been sentenced to a lifetime without the possibility of parole. We were incarcerated by people we love and trust, friends, family, co-workers, ourselves. We go about our daily lives carrying around the shackles of these feelings of unworthiness. We don't reach the goals we want because our chains and walls will not allow it. Our unmanned walls are too high and broad to scale. Or are they?

I have personally struggled with feelings of ineptitude, of not being worthy of anything good in life. These chains were amplified by the fact that I had been incarcerated in a physical prison. I struggled with feeling unworthy of love and acceptance. These walls and chains held me tight and fast. I was depressed and lonely. I didn't feel like I mattered, I was just a waste of space. I was in a solitary confinement doomed to a life sentence without parole. There was no light at the end of my tunnel and no pardon insight. I had no purpose and no meaning. Then, I found the keys to escape.

I am no scholar, nor am I a theologian. I wasn't even a Christian until well into adulthood. I do however know about being in chains and behind walls and fences and how to overcome these obstacles. I am a normal man who made poor choices and landed myself in a prison for almost fifteen years. I served that time and served even longer in a mental prison that my family, society's views, and I created.

Good news! You do not have to live a life of incarceration. You can escape! I have found a process that worked for me, a set of keys if you will. I believe this process can work for you as well. The Lord took pity on me and helped my through my walls and fences. THE SAME CAN HAPPEN FOR YOU!

I felt compelled to write this and share what I went through. My life used to be full of misery, self-loathing, depression. It was a hell I didn't want anyone to go through. I decided to write down the process I went through to break out of my prison. If you have made it this far then you are probably struggling with some of the same type of prisons. You can and you deserve to live a life free of walls and chains. I believe I can help you get there.

Like all things in life this isn't going to be a snap of the fingers. Presto! Chang-o! You are free and happy! It will take work and grit. If you have made it this far in your prison, then your already battle-worn enough for this fight. Continue reading and let's walk the yard through these pages and discuss how we will break you out this joint. Keep your eyes peeled for the guards as we get down to business.

Table of Contents

1. Identify Your Prison

2. Case the Joint

3. Develop Your Escape Plan

4. Train for Freedom

5. Maintain your freedom

6. Conclusion

Chapter 1: Identify Your Prison

People think that a prison is designed to keep hardened criminals at bay. It's a way of protecting our society from heinous acts of violence. That's partly true. In America we have a lot of those. We spend a ton of money to build these and keep them running. There is also prisons with chains and walls that have no financial cost to the taxpayers, but they are effective in keeping down the morale and self-esteem of an untold number of people. These prisons are far more damaging to the people who are incarcerated inside.

Everyone has their own story as to how they became incarcerated in their prisons. Some have spent their lives being told they are worthless, ugly, fat, stupid. Others were made to feel unwelcome and unloved. These words and actions can have a huge and profound effect on a person. It can be even more disastrous if a child deals with this growing up. They grow inside of a prison with walls that get smaller.

I came from a childhood that was troubled like a lot of people. I was a middle child of a divorced couple. I got into trouble at school because my mouth ran non-stop. I had a mother who I am sure loved us but didn't have the necessary skills to raise three boys. A lot of arguing and fighting at home. My mother was also a textbook hoarder, although the term wasn't common back then. My mother would yell everything and had quite the temper. At times she would make comments about how we were," worthless like our father".

Comments like this is how the imprisonment starts. It's a jab that on its own is seems relatively minor, to a seven-year-old boy it hurts badly. More so, because it came from someone who is loved and trusted. When we love and trust someone, we tend to take their words to heart more than that of a stranger we pass on the street. The more we hear things like this the more of your self-esteem gets chipped away at. You start laying the foundation for a prison you don't even realize your building.

Time goes on and things at home became worse. I acted out in school. I ran away a few times thinking that will show mom. She will miss me and when I am back those comments will go away. She will love me again. Things will be fine. Instead I was sent to a therapist because I must have," ran away because I have a something wrong with me. "He needs therapy". So off to the therapist we go.

In my adolescent life I saw several therapist and was told I was suffering from Attention Deficit Disorder by one, Oppressive Defiant Disorder by another, others felt I just had problems expressing myself, or I was just bored in school and that was why I ran my mouth and acted out. All of therapy just reinforced that there is something wrong with me and I am not good enough. Many bricks got laid in those years.

Things progressed and I was sent to a foster home as my mother didn't want me anymore. My dad was nowhere to be found. I ran from those foster homes over-and-over again. This landed me in a group home for kids. More therapist trying to decide what in the world is wrong with this kid. Until finally one day my father showed up. Finally! Someone came to claim me. Someone loves me after all! At least that was my impression at the time.

I moved in with my dad who I quickly learned was stuck in his own battles with Post Traumatic Stress Disorder. In his lucid periods he still commanded his house like he was in still in the military. I learned that I apparently was only good at doing a half-ass job on my chores. After his medication would wane, he would fall into a manic-depressive state and talk about suicide as if it were a foregone conclusion and the world would be better off without him in it. As a pre-adolescent kid this was beyond my understanding. I couldn't figure out why he didn't love me enough to want to be here with me. My prison walls were going up quickly.

I moved in with my dad's sister and her husband as he spent the next few years in a cycle of in and out of the VA hospital. Constantly trying to get his medication and his life back. My aunt and uncle seemed ok at first, they didn't yell or fight during my first month living with them. I suppose they were getting used to me as I was doing the same. One night that all changed. They were arguing, loudly, and it woke me up from a sleep. I came out to the living room to find my uncle hitting my aunt with a closed fist. She was begging him to stop. I ran over and grabbed his left hand, only to be knocked out by hid right cross.

I awoke, blurry vision to my uncle screaming at me that I was nothing but a throw-away kid who better not dare even raise my eyes at him again or he will end my sorry existence. This was more reinforcement of the belief that I was not good, or worthy of love. This time the reinforcement also came with a physical reminder. At this point I was imprisoned. I felt worthless and unloved. I didn't feel as if anyone cared if I lived or died. I just didn't matter at all.

Although I tried to keep a low profile over the next few years there was several more physical altercations and almost daily verbal reminders of my worthlessness. I began not doing my schoolwork or caring. After all I wasn't going to amount to anything anyway. I was just cycling through my days. I was pacing the yard of my mental prison. No hope, nothing to look forward to, I just existed.

My father came back into my life mid-way through my 16 year. I was able to move back with him. By then I was quiet, withdrawn, we didn't speak much. I half-assed my chores, he scolded me, I would shrug and walk away. I existed but that was about all. I watched as he fell off-off his meds and started his spiral downwards. Same-ole, same-ole. He had the thought to send me back with my mom. I hopped on a bus and went back to live with her.

It was clear to me at this point in my life that I must not matter to anyone. After all, I had been told I was worthless repeatedly, the actions of my loved ones showed no one wanted me. Several trained therapists said something was wrong with me, even if they couldn't agree on what that was exactly. Although I couldn't see the bars of my cell, I could sure feel the cold steel against my palms as I grasped them. I was not a normal teenager.

Upon arriving at my mom's house, I had to walk across a sea of garbage that covered the floor. After living with my dad who chewed my butt, for having a pair of socks on the floor, this was a culture shock. I was disgusted. I went to the room I was to sleep in and began to clean. As I took out bag after bag of garbage my resentment and hate grew. The respect one should have for a parent was gone.

We argued often. My little brother, who was a stranger to me, he irritated me beyond explanation. I argued and fought with him as well. In January of 1993 my mom told me I needed to leave. I had nowhere to go and just the clothes on my back as I marched into the frozen town. I struggled to stay warm throughout the nights and couldn't wait until daylight so I could seek shelter in stores and libraries. I was cold, hungry, and quenched my thirst with icicles and snow. I knew I couldn't go on like this for long. My mind frantically raced for a way to get out of this, but my inner voice cried from within its walls that no hope was to be found.

Then out of the darkness of my thoughts another voice began to whisper. Its whispers became louder and soon the words became distinguishable. "You need money, or you will die! You can always rob a bank. It is insured, no one will get hurt. Besides, it is a life or death situation'. That was it, I will rob a bank. If I succeed ill have money to get a place to live. If I fail, I wil at least have a cell and three meals per day.

As the sun rose the next morning I began to plot as I walked around the town and looked for a possible bank to rob. I finally settled on one on the southwest side of town. It was small, a block off the main road. It didn't appear to have any security officers to guard it. This is the one. The problem I had to figure out was; how to ensure the police wouldn't get to the bank before I could get away. A flash back memory from when I was in school came to mind. Call in a bomb threat.

I spent the next freezing evening trying to ignore my hunger pains. I ran the bank robbery through my head over, and over again. I needed a gun, I had nowhere to find one. Instead I would go to a grocery store and steal a toy gun, I would use that to pull off the job.

I was sick to my stomach at first but the more my stomach growled the more I felt more comfortable with the idea. As the sun came upon the horizon I was set. I was going to rob this bank or get caught trying. Either way I would have a roof over my head and food in my stomach by days end.

The next morning, I went to the local grocery store and sure enough, they had a toy isle. I looked but the only realistic gun they had was one with a bright orange tip. I picked it up. I looked once, twice, and down the front of my pants the gun disappeared. I walked over to the paper supplies and found a black sharpie. Perfect. Down the front of my pants it went as well.

I slowly made my way outside and ran. Stopping a few blocks later I pulled the gun from its package. I couldn't get the orange tip to come off. I pulled out the black sharpie and began to go over the tip. Changing the blaze orange to a black solid mass. This will have to do.

I watched from a block away as the workers arrived at the bank. Once the Man inside unlocked the doors I walked over to a pay phone and dialed 911. I tried to deepen my voice as I said, "There is a bomb inside the JCPenney store North of town. I hung up the phone and waited. Moments later I watched as several emergency personnel whirled past me. I listened until I could no longer hear the sirens.

Show time! I struggled to pull myself together and walked across the street and entered the bank. There was an empty plastic grocery store bag in the garbage can. I pulled it out and walked over to the counter with the withdrawal and deposit slips. I grabbed an ink pen and a withdrawal slip and began to write on the back. I don't recall what I wrote exactly, but it was to the extent of, "put the money in the bag and no one gets hurt". My hands shook while I wrote.

I turned towards the counter to find a woman greeting me with a smile. "I can help you", she said. I walk toward the smiling lady, legs feeling like lead weights attached. My heart thundering inside of my chest. I reached out with my note and handed it to her. As she read the note a look of confusion and fear swept across her face. My left hand, hands her the bag as my right pulls out the toy gun to expose it to her. She is noticeably shaking as she empty's the contents of her till into the plastic bag and hands it back to me.

I push the gun back into my waist band and grab the bag and try to force myself to walk as I make my way to the door.

The fresh cold air from outside hits my face and I am off like a panther across the parking lot. 'I can't believe I just robbed a bank', I thought. My feet hit the street and I hear an audible, 'HISSSSSS'! I look down at the bag as I run and see it filling up with red smoke. I had never seen one, but immediately knew what the smoke was. Die bomb! I chuck it to the ground and continue running. I did an act out of desperation and destroyed my life and had nothing to show for it.

As you can guess I was caught and imprisoned. Now my body was as imprisoned as my mind. It's ironic that the physical imprisonment wasn't anywhere near as hurtful as the prison I was living in inside my mind. I am sure a lot of people can relate to that.

Anyone being told they are less worthy of love, or less attractive than others, or worthless has a battle in front of them. It can affect your self-image and self-worth. Being demeaned by loved ones who are supposed to protect and nourish you can have horrific results on the development of an adolescent.

Adults however are also not immune to this kind of assault. The longer people experience this the more it chips away at self-worth, and the faster your prison is built. Until such a time as you cannot see the light of day. You become truly incarcerated and your heart and mind are imprisoned.

In my prison cell I would put up pictures of mountains, tropical islands, pictures of animals on the wall. I would take my bed sheets and hang them over my bars, so I wasn't looking into the hallway or at guards walking the hallways. All of this was a distraction.

Out in society we have video games, computers, face-book, television to keep our minds distracted. These distractions cover up the walls much like my magazine cut-outs on the walls, but it doesn't change the fact that the walls still exist, and the bars covered with bedsheets are still just as present.

We tend to distract ourselves because we don't want to feel the pain of our incarceration. If we can avoid it or distract ourselves for even a second, then we do just that. We seek a moment of reprieve. Let's face it, no one wants to feel unworthy, or ugly, or worthless and depressed. We look for ways to distract our brains and hearts from the pain. If we stop, then these thoughts and emotions come flooding back. We are avoiding not only the problem but also our way to any possible release.

My first step to my release was to be quiet. My form of quiet came the hard way. I was in a maximum-security prison after escaping a prison center and being recaptured in 1996. It was seven years after being recaptured and all was not well with me. I was in the lowest of lows.

I was walking to the chow hall hating everyone and everything. As I grabbed my tray the chow-hall officer monitoring the kitchen staff said something I took offense too. I rattled back some obscenity and proceeded to walk away.

That when I heard him mumble, "I'd beat you're a## you f-'ing punk". The tray dropped from my hand ass I jumped over the serving line and began striking the corrections officer repeatedly. Moments later I had multiple guards on top of me, trying to take me to the ground.

I held onto the lip of the serving line as one guard tried to shove my head into the pan of canned baked beans. It is funny how I can still smell the beans even to this day. After moments of struggle the guards had me cuffed and were leading me out of the chow-hall towards the administrative segregation unit.

When I got to the ad seg unit they put me into a cell on base gallery and three officers piled in behind me rang down blows onto head chest and shoulders. I struggled to break my handcuffs to get my hands in front of me but to no avail. I kicked out with my leg trying to strike back and head butted one guard. They finally retreated and slammed the door shut and locked me in. I spent the next twelve hours cuffed in the cell. I finally calmed down.

It was a different shift of guards who came to take me to a different cell. They got me inside and took off my handcuffs and gave me a bedroll. I was exhausted and bruised from head to toe. I thought that was the end, but it wasn't. I spent the next ten days with no food. The guards would come to my cell and act as if they would give me a food tray then laugh and walk on by. I ate a tube of toothpaste sparingly hoping I could survive on that.

The morning of day eleven I was beyond starving and visibly looking like I was knocking on deaths door. Then as the breakfast trays were passed out a tray of oatmeal was placed on my food slot and the guard walked away. I was starving and never in my life did a tray of bland oatmeal smell so good. I reached for it anxiously. I was sure they had spit in it or done something to the food, but I was so hungry I didn't care. I gobbled it up in seconds.

After breakfast the security officers took me to the control center where the state police were there to book me on assault charges. Now it all made sense. They fed me so I couldn't tell the state trooper I was being starved to death. I tried to tell the trooper, but he told me the deputy warden told him I was refusing my food and I was on a hunger strike. I had no ground to stand on.

Over the next year I was sentenced to an additional 1-4-year sentence for punching the guard. Year number two in the hole I was in a routine of pacing my cell, going to the segregation yard, A.K.A. ,dog kennels, and pacing while trying not to get hit by feces as the mentally ill inmates had poop wars with each other and the guards.

At night you fell asleep listening to the screams of inmates as the slowly lost their minds and slammed their steel foot-locker lids against the wall and back down again, over and over and over.

I sat their wishing for an end to the nightmare I was living. I had never made a point to talk to God, but I was desperate and reached out. Hoping for some response. No angel appeared before me or visions or anything spectacular. Instead it was an inner feeling of what I needed to do. I needed to quiet myself and the feeling was so strong that I did just that. I laid on my pad on top of my concrete slab and just sat still.

I didn't know what to expect or what I should do so I sat. I got bored. My mind raced with fantasies of grandeur. I daydreamed about shooting the winning goal in the Olympic games. I fantasized about being given a pardon and handed ten million dollars from a relative I had never heard of. My thoughts eventually went where they always went. To the dark and loathsome self-hatred. I tried to expel them to go back to distractions of fantasy, but to no avail. I finally felt the need to listen to my own thoughts in truth.

Thus far I had no idea I was on a journey to my freedom. I was in solitary-confinement, I had just gotten an addition to my sentence. I was close to losing my sanity and now some random voice was telling me to basically shut up and listen to my thought s in truth. Whatever that meant. I was on a ride, but all signs pointed south at the time. What is going on?

Truth is a hard concept for a lot of people. We are inundated with lies every day. Politicians lie, Preachers are lying on tax returns, parents lie to kids about make believe people who leave money for teeth and who magically give out presents to good boys and girls. Lies are everywhere and it becomes easy to lie to ourselves. The truth however is harder to swallow, unless it's something we have already told ourselves and we believe. That's a nice sugar-coated pill we get behind.

I couldn't wrap my brain around having any problem with myself. I gave in and listened to the inner feeling of listening to my thoughts in truth. I examined how I felt about guards. I didn't like them. Why? I don't know they are keeping me here. I didn't like my family. Why? They abandoned me. Who did I like or love? ….. No answer came. Why don't I love anyone? They don't love me. Is that true? Well yeah, just look at how I was treated. Is it that they didn't love you or that they don't have the skills to love and raise kids? Perhaps they have their own issues they are struggling with? Do you not love because how you were treated, and your own self- issues stunted your abilities?

I questioned my own thoughts and feelings in the quiet and although I made excuses the more I sat quietly in truth, the more truth I found in my thoughts. Things were still a jumble, but I had this weird sense that things were starting to click. I didn't want to admit it, but maybe this inner voice/feeling might be onto something.

Before I knew it, I was spending time daily in my quiet truth. Reflecting on what random point my brain would go to that day. If nothing else I felt a little less hateful. Not much but maybe a little. A slight change was better than the status quo that I was living in from day to day.

For me, it took an extreme event to happen to drive me to a rock bottom situation. A lot of people outside of prison have their own rock bottom situations going on every day. It doesn't take going to prison and segregation to sit down in quiet reflection. Turn off the phones, computers, video games. Listen to your thoughts in truth.

In my quiet reflection, I began to struggle with the why's. Why am I so worthless? Why am I so horrible that no one loves me? Why am I such a piece of garbage? Why do I make such poor decisions? Why don't I care about other people? The struggles with the why's made me want to break down. More's why came up. Why can't I cry? Why aren't I empathetic? This thought process made me miserable and I began to think this was a waste of time. Funny because time was the only thing, I had plenty of. The why questions were essential.

As I sat in my solitary-confinement I prepared to go out to the seg-yard/dog kennels to pace. The guard on duty announced over the inner com that if the inmates would refuse to go outside to the segregation yard, they would turn on the cable for the unit. A lot of inmates had 12 inch black and white televisions. There was no cable in segregation. This was a rare treat. I was going from zero television stations to twenty-six!

I watched T.V. all day. What an escape! I scanned through the channels and I heard a guitar rhythm on I.N.S.P. It was a commercial for the top ten count-down. My first reaction was what kind of Christian music is this? It sounded like normal music. I thought may as well check it out as it was coming on. I watched the count-down and the number one song was "Savior" by the band,

"Skillet". I didn't have the word's memorized, but the rhythm stuck in my head. At shift change the guards turned off the cable and I was serenaded by the screams of the rest of the inmates.

I thought about the day's events and the shows I watched, and I began humming the rhythm to the Skillet song. I went back to my quiet reflection in truth, but my mind drifted to God. I started talking to him in my mind. As I talked to Him, I began reflecting on my why questions. It came to me that I wasn't just physically in prison. My mind and emotions were imprisoned as well. My why questions changed into how. How did I become imprisoned?

This question took a long time to ponder. I took a hard look at my life. I examined the relationships I had with everyone I could possibly think of. I searched the depths of my memory to recall every bad or negative thing that was said to me. Every insult that reinforced the feeling of self-doubt and poor self-image. I finally started to understand. I built the walls to my prison. I built the bars, and the Constantine wire fence around it. I did this in a vain attempt to protect myself.

The human body is a wonderous and strange thing. If you freezing to death the body cuts circulation to the extremities to protect the vital organs. Likewise, our sub-conscience tries to protect us from perceived threats. We put up walls and fences to distance ourselves from hurtful comments from people. Yet these walls don't always keep the harmful words out. In time these hurtful words and experiences we go through tend to become truths to us. Instead of our walls protecting us, they keep these negative thoughts and self-images locked up inside our prisons with us.

We become imprisoned with our thoughts and perceived faults. Instead of being protected we become engrossed in a world of self-negatives. These thoughts and feelings are locked up with us. They become our cell mates. We live, eat, and sleep with them. It is no wonder we become attached to these thoughts and feelings. We spend all our time with them and develop a close relationship.

Our walls and fences are up and our fortress is strong. It is hard to form significant relationships with others. It's difficult to open -up and put ourselves out there. We can't truly enjoy life and other people because we can't truly see and feel because our walls, fences and chains hold us at bay. We have an army of guards standing in the way. Houston, we have a problem!

Like all problems, we first acknowledge we have a problem before we can fix it. If we don't reflect and learn the truth of our situation, we will never discover we are in a bad way. After our quiet reflection and listening to our truth, we need to figure out how we got in our situation. With this self-discovery we find that we have a problem. Once we know we have put ourselves into a prison of negative self-images and perceptions and realize how it affects our lives we can work on a plan to escape this and solve our problem.

When I was released from prison I thought, "that's it I am free"! Little did I know I was still incarcerated. My quiet reflection was great. I knew I was in a prison of negatives. I still had not figured out that it was not tied to my being in prison with the state of Michigan. I thought I was free, and life will be sunshine and rainbows. Surprise. Surprise. It was not that way at all.

I struggled. I mean struggled. I got some public assistance for food and a 100-dollar voucher for clothes at the Goodwill store. I pounded the pavement trying to get a job. Any job. Door after door was slammed in my face. I lost count of the times that I was told," we don't hire criminals". Literally I applied at every business I saw. I even filled out applications at funeral homes. I was desperate for any kind of work.

The old thoughts crept back into my mind. You are still worthless. No one wants you. No one cares. Your just an evil criminal. I was still imprisoned. I went to a church seeking guidance. I was met with a polite smile but the pastor I spoke to was not at all welcoming.

I felt ashamed as I talked to him and his looks told me he was just placating me by listening. I found my way out of there and talked to myself on the way home. I cussed at myself and eventually I found my quiet reflection. As I walked I eventual talked angrily to God. After I vented, I started to have that inner feeling guiding me to the truth about my prison walls on my heart and mind.

I was never going to be free if I didn't acknowledge that this prison of negatives, I was locked up, with was a barrier affecting every aspect of my life. It was the problem that needed to be acknowledged, if I hoped to ever be free. I stopped at a park on the way home and sat on a bench." I am stuck and I need help", I pleaded. "Everything I do is affected by my thoughts and feelings, nothing I do works. I don't feel worthy of love and respect. I am in chains behind a wall of hurt and unworthiness. I need you, please help me find a way out! God please help me"! I had finally acknowledged that I had a problem.

A breakthrough had taken place. Like a drug-addict finally accepting his abuse, I had acknowledged that I had a problem and needed to change if I was to ever break free of this status quo life.

Chapter Overview:

- A lot of people suffer from self-incarceration. Whether is low self-esteem or poor self-image.

- Honest Self-reflection can lead to understanding the true nature of the problem.

- Accept the truth of your self-reflections.

- Admitting you have a problem is the first step in escaping from self-incarceration.

Chapter 2: Case the Joint

People can be stubborn. They tend to resist change. It is scary for them. People don't like to change themselves and they are not a fan of other people changing. The only constant thing is life is change. To resist change is to resist nature and the fabric of our reality. We are changing from the day we are conceived until the day we pass. I am no different than anyone else. I didn't admit I had a problem, ask for help, and Poof! Life was grand!

I really struggled with who was keeping me captive in my mental and emotional prison. I really did think, "Well, I don't want to be here, I want to be free. SO, let's go! What is the hold up on my release paperwork? I should be out of this isolation by now!" I was still stuck inside. I hadn't dealt with any issues.

I just knew I was still inside walls. I wanted to be free, but I wasn't.

When I was sitting in long term administrative-segregation I wanted to be free. I fantasized about freedom. I had a yearning to be free, but I still sat surrounded by four walls and what seemed like endless isolation. My own thoughts kept me company. As I waited.

Like my mental prison I started a quiet self-reflection and listened to my truth. I realized my actions against others was keeping me from making any headway on any sort of release from ad-seg. I decided that if I was ever going to get out of the hole, (segregation), I would need to change something. I decided I needed something positive to occupy my time and that was a visual clue to the guards that something was different about me. Something for the better.

I had always tinkered with art, but I couldn't draw a stick figure, let alone something worthy of people enjoying. I decided to give soap carving a try. I had a paper clip in my legal documents and plenty of soap. I started by finding small clip art pictures that I would place on a bar of soap and trace the design over the paper leaving an indentation in the soap. From there, I would try to turn it into a 3-D version. The first few attempts weren't the best. However, I had time on my side. I kept it up. Pretty soon the things I made were good replicas of the pictures.

The first few times going to the segregation showers after I started carving soap, I would come back to my sculptures having been confiscated. The guards didn't write me up for this, but they took my pieces. I continued to make them. After a while, I became bored with making small soap-art.

I started experimenting with crushing soap down into small pieces and using water to make clay. The small pieces wouldn't hold. I crushed it into powder and finally I had the recipe for larger artwork. No soap is extremely fragile in a soft state and I learned from trial and error that you would have to make braces as it dried to hold it up. I would make basic childish forms and use my paperclip to bring out the details. The guards became curious and would leave my projects and ask me what I was making.

After time I started getting request from guards to make items for their kids. A deputy warden once asked me to make a motorcycle. I complied. Not because I got anything in return, but the left me alone to pass my time. Shortly after I realized that not only did my days go by faster, but my mood was elevated. I had a purpose and reason for getting up each day and I was showing that I could do something positive with myself.

As I approached another anniversary in segregation I was brought before the review board. Shockingly, the guards had recommended my release back into general population. I was back in general population with freedom, or as much as you can have in a maximum-security prison. I at least got to walk to a chow-hall instead of being fed inside my cell. I was able to go outside for one hour a day in a bigger dog kennel. Baby-steps.

Word of my soap carving s spread to the inmates and I was able to make a few prison bucks making items for inmates to send to their loved ones. I made quite a bit of prison cash, (Honeybun's, ramen noodles, toothpaste and stamps, and so on). I got into painting my sculptures with common items. I used instant coffee mixed with floor sealant I got from the porters/janitors. I took the lead from water soluble colored pencils and expanded my color palate. I took time but I got good at painting with Q-tips and my homemade paints. I cut out pictures from magazines and newspaper ads in the Sunday paper, so I knew what colors cartoon characters were. Afterall, black and white televisions don't explain colors all that well.

I continued carving soap and noticed that my thoughts turned into a mental dialogue with God as I carved soap. I would have my mental conversations and carve until my fingers hurt from holding the paperclip. You would think this was be a deterrent, but it was a pleasant pain. Before long I had thoughts and daydreams of carving out of clay and selling pieces out-side in the real world.

I recognized that my attitude and actions was there reasons for my added time and imprisonment. Putting effort into something positive, I eventually got back positive things. I made, a decision. I would do something to better my situation and started acting on it. I had acknowledged the problem was me. Being homeless at seventeen wasn't the problem. I could have made another choice. I was in the hole because of my choices. I was the problem and once I accepted that I was ready to move on to the next step.

In the mental prison, I too was the person holding me inside. I told to myself I wanted to be free. I spoke it convincingly, as I clutched the chains in a death grip to my chest. I was lying to myself. I was not willing to put forth any effort to change. I blamed the issues I went through as a child but did nothing to deal with those issues to move forward. I held the walls of my prison securely in place.

People tend to stand in their own way. The biggest enemy you face, aside from the devil, is yourself. I am my own worst enemy. It has taken me a very long time to figure this out. I used to lie to myself that it was other people's issues. Once I finally acknowledged that I was the problem I had to figure out if I wanted to be free. I was held captive so long that being in a prison of my own mind was a comfort. Like a child with a blankie. I held onto this blankie of steel and concrete for comfort.

Freedom comes with a price. Our founding fathers fought like a banshee to secure our freedom in the new world. Our soldiers battle across the globe to eliminate threats to maintain our freedom. The cost they pay is lost time with family, surviving facing mortality, mental and emotional anguish, possible loss of life. Yet, they pay that cost because freedom is important to them and our way of life. I It should come as no surprise there would be a price to pay to secure a freedom from your prison. In order to be free of your imprisonment you have too want to be free and be ready to pay a price for that freedom as well.

Escape Your Prisons

As I sat, in my cell, carving soap, I realized if I ever hoped to be free, to set feet outside of prison and have any semblance of a normal life, I would have to truly want to be free.. I had to decide, if that was what I wanted, and if I was committed to follow through. My physical prison was a place, I was all about getting away from. My mental prison I thought, was because I was physically bound.

I needed to commit, to wanting my freedom. Saying you want freedom and committing to freedom are two very different deals. One is a thought and one is action. I needed to stop thinking about being free and start putting something into action to if I ever hoped to get out of the Michigan Department of Corrections, (M.D.O.C.).

I had no idea of what the necessary steps were to eventual be released from the Michigan Department of Corrections. I started with not arguing with people, which led to me getting a prison job in the health care unit as a porter., I finished my schooling by getting my General Education Diploma, (G.E.D.). I occupied myself with activities like reading, I started going to church, and yes, carving soap. By all appearances I was transitioning into a person who could be rehabilitated. Until roadblocks appeared.

My first significant roadblock came in a prison chapel. I had an on-off relationship with God. I tried reading the bible like a book but was stuck on the lineage in the old testament. I didn't understand point of it. Nor, did I understand the love of God when the old testament was more of a wrathful God.

This was where I decided to go to church. Afterall all the grand people in society go to church. Perhaps ill gain understanding there.

I signed up for services and started to gain some perspective on God the trinity. I spoke more often with him and felt a change in my heart. As time went on, I noticed that church services for other inmates was just a time to get out of their cell and for the prison homosexuals to pass love notes and cop a feel. I was sickened. As a new Christian I believed this was supposed to be a holy place and I didn't feel like God was here at service with me.

To make matters worse I started to not understand how I could read a passage and understand it to mean X+Y=Z, yet the pastor was saying X+Y=A. It didn't make sense to me. I started to bounce to different denominational services and got the same conclusion. Sure, the basis of faith was the same, but how to live as a Christian varied depending on what service you went to. Bible verses were thrown out like candy and all it did was confuse me all-the-more. The congregation hollered Amen at anything that was said. Was I the only one that thought about was being said? All this put doubts in my head. I decided to stop going to service. I didn't feel God there anyway.

I went through a time of not feeling Gods presence, but I also didn't go out of my way to seek him either. We talked from time to time, but I noticed it was like an old friend separated from you. The distance between calls gets farther apart as time goes on. I started feeling anxious and angry. I stopped feeling like I should try to do better.

Sometimes all it takes is a reminder of something good to set you back on the right track. For me, that reminder came in the form of a Christian parable in a free publication I received in the mail. I don't remember the publication's name or the author, but the story stuck in my head.

The story went something like, "A beggar in rags stood on the steps to the church weeping, Jesus came down and asked, What's wrong? The beggar replied that they won't let me in because of my tattered clothes and dirty face. Jesus replied, "don't feel bad they don't let me in either".

Whatever the thought process and authors intention, this helped me to regain focus and return-back on my path of trying to get out of the M.D.O.C. I figured that even if I don't fully understand the goings on in the prison Chapel, I should not neglect my relationship with God.

Things started to pay off as my custody level dropped from a level 5 maximum security to a level 4 medium security. More yard and dayroom time. More opportunities to improve on myself. I continued-on-a-path of action and was eventually rewarded a drop in custody again, which led to a parole and a release in 2009.

I still struggled with my mental and emotional prisons. After my triumphant return of me to society, I was still imprisoned. As I sat on that park bench and acknowledged my problem, I also committed to wanting to be released. I pleaded to God for help. I offered a commitment of heart and soul to be free regardless of sacrifice. I was now truly committed to wanting my freedom.

It took more than a passive wish to be free from my inner Hell to start the process of escape. I needed to have a firm and committed will that was dead set on breaking out of this joint or it would never work. There would be no half-ass to this. It was all or nothing. After all, the years of living a torturous life inside my own heart and mind, I had finally drawn the conclusion that I had, finally had enough. I would do whatever it takes to get out. I just needed to be shown the way.

My experience with God was not a, I talk, and he directly replied with an audible voice. His responses with me were more inner-feelings and insights. Some may argue that these are self-epiphany's, or your own thoughts. You can take this how you choose. I believe these revelations were from God, revelations given through the Holy Spirit. If you believe otherwise, so be it. Free will is God's gift to all men. Since this is my book, I will continue through my experience and let all develop their own opinion, which I would love to hear. I'll leave my contact details in end of this book for you.

Now that we acknowledged that we are holding ourselves in prison, and we are committed to making an escape, its time to really think about what to do next. We want to be successful we may only get one shot. This could be our do or die moment. Like any great prison break you don't just charge the fence. The odds of being shot in the back while climbing are much higher than successfully getting over. We need to first gather some information. We need to case the joint.

Casing the joint will be nonchalant. No one wants attention drawn to their self while in this process. No sense giving the guards a warning that you are up to something. You're going to gain information as you go about your daily lives. By all appearances, you are just doing the same-ole stuff just another day. Secretly you will be in a state of analyzing.

You need to walk the yard and figure out what kind of security fences we must scale. Look for any weakness's that we can utilize. Where are the guards watching and waiting to shut us down? Are there any snitches or roadblocks to avoid?

I had put up some pretty high walls in my prison with a double row of Constantine wire. I knew that if I was going to ever scale those walls, I would have to have a serious look at how they got there in the beginning. (This is where the quiet reflection comes back into play.) I had to examine in depth, the situations that led to building these walls. I had to revisit these situations and log them, so they could be addressed later. Without examining them closely how could you ever hope to climb them later?

Locating the location and number of guards holding me hostage in my mind and heart took some painstaking research. I had to examine my thoughts and define what specific thoughts are keeping me inside these walls. What triggers these thoughts? Damaging thoughts can sometimes be generic like a guard who is dressed in civilian clothes acting as a case manager/counselor. They seem innocent and trustful, but, are every bit a guard keeping you locked down. Knowing where they are and how to deal with them would be vital for escape.

The snitches. Oh my, beware of the snitches. These are the people that claim to be your friend or mellow. They eat with you, smile and joke with you. Claim to be down for you and love you. All the while they are holding you back by sliding information to your prison officials. They are the people who you think care but are full of negativity and feed your self-doubt the bricks and mortar to build walls. They have their own agenda's. They are all about making their situations better at your expense.

It is a lot of work to gain the information you need to facilitate you're your escape. It will be a challenge and heart wrenching at times. Remember, you can do this! Look at what you have gone through and survived. Look at your feet standing firmly on the ground. It may not seem like it, but headway is being made. You did a lot of the work. You acknowledged how you got inside and who is keeping you locked down. You decided it was time to escape.

Casing the joint to find the weakness of your prison, identifying, guards, snitches can seem daunting, but you are a battle worn convict that can handle this process. Hell has been your companion, and your prepared to fight for freedom. Let's take this a step further. Now let's make an escape plan. I was more dedicated than ever of breaking my prison to provide a better life and to be a role model for my son.

Chapter Overview:

- Self-reflection or quiet truth can help expose the weaknesses of your prisons.
- Identify the people, thoughts, and triggers that have you putting up walls.
- Accept the things you suffered through in life. It happened.
- Deal with past hurt.
- Understand you will be tried and face setbacks. It is okay. You are human after all.

Chapter 3: TRAIN FOR ESCAPE

How do I escape? That is, "the ten-million-dollar question,". Every convict wants to know. It isn't an easy answer. If it were, then no one would be left in prison. Every inmate would have already been long gone, sitting on a beach somewhere in a country like Belize, that has no extradition. Good news! We have the answer to the how to escape. It isn't easy but we have the tools and are ready to develop our plan.

Once I had made up my mind that I had a problem and made the determination that I was ready to be free of my inner hell, I started the process of, escaping. I cased the joint and found who the snitches were. that were reporting to my mental prison officials. I located the thought/guards that were holding me back. Now it was time to start putting together the plan.

I had to break down my barriers one by one. I started with the guards. The thoughts that were negative, full of self-hate and self-loathing had to be dealt with. In order to do that I had to deal with the past. You were hurt by the people you loved. This hurt led to thoughts and feelings that put you down, and made you feel devalued and unloved. These thoughts of not being worthy or less important than others are not real. These consuming thoughts are a constant thorn in your mind and heart that needs to be removed, the hole replaced with positive things.

I had plenty of negative thoughts in my life. Plenty of my life situations led to an all-consuming feeling and thought of being less than equal to my fellow man. I had friends, family and guards who all told me I was worthless. I had a stream of failures that backed up these feelings and thoughts. It was up to me to make-an-effort to throw out these thoughts and replace the hole left behind with thoughts of being worthy of good.

As I started dealing with the people in my life that told me I was not worthy, I started to realize that this was not my baggage. It was there's. I didn't do anything to justify being told I was worthless and less important then another. These people in my life that made these comments and treated me poorly had issues of their own. Much like sexual abuse can be passed down through generations, so can coping skills, and verbal and physical abuse.

I didn't realize this way back then, but at last I had figured things out. We cannot choose the family we are born into, and we can't make people change for the better. Only they can do that. We can however choose how we deal with these people after we realize that they have unresolved issues and they are dealing with things they way they were either taught or figured out on their own.

The negative, self-loathing, thoughts however, was on me to deal with. I had to get real with myself and really look at these thoughts that led to the way I acted or reacted.

I examined these thoughts one by one. I needed to replace the negative with positive thoughts. As the negative thoughts came up, I had to make a conscious effort to slap them down and replace them. If I started to feel like I wasn't good enough, I had to stop and say, "Enough! I am good enough. I do deserve to be treated with respect and kindness".

This is not a one-time process. These thoughts will pop up over-and-over again. It takes vigilance to monitor your thoughts and to be on guard to replace these thoughts as they come up. It is an ongoing process. There will be times you won't truly believe the replacement thoughts. Fake it until you make it! As time goes on, it becomes easier. Soon it becomes, not only habit to have positive thoughts, but you will find that the negative thoughts become fewer and farther between.

This was something I needed guidance on. I reached out to God for guidance and help. I struggled with faith as it was relayed to me by preachers and chaplains. I noticed that there was no cookie cutter words a preacher could say to reach every individual. For me, I had to really didn't feel God's presence in church.

Yet when I looked out and saw the tree's, sky, moon, and sun. I felt Him. When I saw animals and the grandeur of our world. I felt Him. This is when I talked the most to God. His presence reflected in my thoughts and I soon felt change.

This is not meant to be overtly religious, but this is my tale of how I came to escape my self-incarceration. God played a role in my life and I believe he worked through me granting me guidance and insight. No judgement for those who believe or do not. We all hold the keys to our own salvation. Moving on.

I had eventually found a job as a groundskeeper for the local college. I made $8.35 per hour and rarely got overtime. I replaced the constant negative thoughts with positive, even though I didn't feel it. The fact that I had gotten any kind of a job was a baby step in the direction of something more positive then what I had in the past.

I had to focus on the small positives in life. Soon I had more and more positives. I had a girlfriend and a baby while I was on parole. I was able to find a different lawn care related job that paid $10.00 per hour. A step up in the right direction.

Life wasn't all peachy. I still had bills I couldn't pay. Back then, I had to decide which bill was more important, then pay the bill that was more of a necessity. The food budget got cut the most and I would survive on Great Value chicken breast, Ramen noodles, and peanut butter. Steak and hamburger were luxuries I couldn't really afford, much like soda, and milk.

The reoccurring self-doubt would creep in, but I was still vigilante, forcing those thoughts aside and re-focusing on the positive aspects in my life. Wouldn't you know, life comes along and change things up and throw you a few curve balls when you least expect.

My definition of hell changed the day my son was born. I was filled with the biggest sense of joy and happiness. Moments later nurses and doctors were scrambling, my son was whisked away to the infant intensive care unit. My mind was a whirl as I asked the staff for answers. My son was born with Downs Syndrome, and Dandy Walker Syndrome. The Dandy-Walker Syndrome is water on the brain. If the fluid becomes too much, it can cause all kinds of problems like seizures, strokes and potentially death. He also had a hole in his heart and a potential heart surgery was up in the air.

The staff pulled me outside the operating room to talk to me. They explained the potential complications that could happen and that they needed to monitor my son closely. As my girlfriend was sent to a recovery room, I was escorted to the Infant Intensive Care Unit, (N.I.C.U.). My son sat in a plastic bed that looked like a clear tote on wheels. It seemed like a hundred different wires and tubes were attached to his tiny little body. There were twenty or so other plastic beds like his in the room. Each one holding a baby with just as many wires and tubes.

I spent my overnights in the N.I.C.U. and left the hospital to go to work during the day. I prayed and talked to God almost every waking minute begging for the health and safety of my son. I was beyond exhausted. On the fourth day as I left the hospital to make the thirty-minute commute to work. I was driving and for whatever reason, the shadow of a telephone pole across the highway, I thought was a steel wire strewn across the road at head height.

I locked up the brakes on the car to avoid what seemed like certain death. As my car stopped, I realized that I needed sleep and soon! I finished my shift and went back to the hospital. After checking on my son I went to my girl-friends room and passed out in the chair.

I maybe slept a total of twenty hours in that ten-day period. The bags under my eyes were green and I resembled something from a zombie movie. I witnessed countless family's struggle with their own children's health issues. It broke my heart whenever I came to the N.I.C.U and saw a bed that was empty, as I knew the reason was most likely horrendous.

Pain and fear were mask's every parent wore. Eyes were red and blood shot from crying and lack of sleep. None of the suffering I went through came close to this. The other parents and I were bounded by a pain and suffering few will ever know. The staff you came to know on a first name basis. Yet I was extremely lucky.

Escape Your Prisons

My son improved and I had guilt. I was beyond happy that God took pity on me, yet I hurt inside and felt guilty because I watched to many other parents have to say goodbye to a life that barely lived. You could clearly see the toll it took on the N.I.C.U. staff. They put on a brave face for the parents but more than once I saw them break down at the nurse station. The suffering of lives cut short was felt by more than just the families. After this my personal problems seemed miniscule. God put my life into perspective. Whether I wanted it to be or not.

Remaining positive and replacing thoughts is an ongoing challenge that is made more difficult by changes in your life. There will be times you won't feel positive or will allow your old thoughts to creep back into your mind. That is okay! You are only human. If this happens recognize your thoughts, regain your composure and forcefully replace those thoughts with the positives you do have in your life. It takes time and practice. Eventually you will fake it enough that it starts to become a habit. Soon it becomes ever easier to do this and you will find that the negative thoughts come fewer and farther between.

Nothing worthwhile in life comes easy. These words are oh, so, true. It takes determination and a strong will to fight for something you want. Your will, will be tested and tried. Relax, you are battle-worn from years of fighting inside your prison. You have the gust-o, to take on this challenge. Like an inmate scraping a shank on the concrete floor of his cell, get ready to sharpen the edges of your will for the battle against your thoughts. This battle could be a full-scale war at times. It may be long and drawn out. But sticking to your guns will prove you victorious in the end.

During my time as a released inmate I battled to not only maintain my freedom but to also overcome my self-inflicted obstacles. Not all, of the obstacles I faced were of my own doing. I faced a lot of push-back from people in society as well. I had employers who wanted to keep me labeled as no good because of my criminal past. I had people who wouldn't allow me to volunteer my time for charity's because they saw me as a no-good ex-con. I had to be determined to succeed and move forward despite these obstacles and despite of anyone who thought otherwise.

When I was released, I was barely able to get a job and even then, I struggled to find anything that paid more than minimum wage. I kept searching and after being rejected hundreds of times I was able to get employed for an oil rig company. I started as a worm on a work-over rig in Hobbs, New Mexico. Shortly after, I was transferred to North Dakota as the oil boom was on in the Bakken. After a few years on the rigs I started noticing the toll the job took on my body. Afterall, most people started this in their early 20's and here I was breaking into the industry at 32.

I decided to make a switch and went to work for a oilfield support company. After I was told I had the job I was called back to the office. When I arrived, I sat in front of the area Manager and operations manager, with the head Human Resource Manager on conference call. The Human Resource manager had gotten back my background check and had concerns.

They told me they could see that I had a checkered past and asked me to explain. Simply put I told them I would not explain as my past didn't define who I am as a person, especially something that took place almost 20 years prior. I further explained that if this company felt that this defined me then it wasn't a company I wanted to work for.

Apparently, my answer pleased them because I got the job. It wasn't long before my strong work ethic and steadfastness won them over. Soon opinions started to change for them about what kind of people ex-cons can become.

It is at this point I realized that new challenges were inevitable. Not only did I have to deal with past issues and heartache, but new challenges were being thrown at me at an alarming rate. I had to stay vigilant and not allow myself to be pigeon-toed into a category of unworthiness by others.

I was dead set that I would be the person I wanted to be, and to be-seen-as the person I now understood that I was. Not a worthless human, but a person that had value, and deserved to be treated with dignity, respect. One that was worthy of love and kindness.

Chapter Overview:

- Dark Thoughts will try to return.

- New challenges will appear trying put you back inside your prison.

- Be vigilant to dark thoughts. Replace them with positive thought.

- Defend your freedom.

CHAPTER 4: Train for Freedom

As an inmate, you get good at finding ways to avoid guards and places where you might be on camera or under someone's watchful eye. Inside there is an entire world of underground deals and activity that takes place daily on prison yards. In order, for your prison enterprise to stay going, you need to be good at avoiding guards. Let's take a page out of that book to help us train for our freedom.

Of the time I spent with my own thoughts, one thing I noticed was that I allowed myself to be in situations that led to unnecessary hurt and or hurtful thought patterns. I had to become mindful of these guards. As I found these in my life, I had to recognize them and avoid those situations that led to my thoughts turning towards the darkness. This may be difficult. It could mean avoiding people and situations that you have grown accustomed to being around. They may even be loved ones that you need to avoid for a period-of-time.

After being released from prison and starting my transition for release from my mental prison, I began avoiding old situations and people that fed into the building of my personal prison. I had a lot of things to avoid. Certain family members became the first of my avoidance. Which only makes sense given their track record in my life.

The family members in my life that promoted negativity, I had to avoid. Not because I didn't love or care for them, but because I was in a newly released state and didn't want to be encouraged to rebuild my prison or be subjected to comments that would lead to negative thoughts.

I made a conscious decision to avoid anything that didn't reflect positivity. If it was negative in nature, it was tossed out of my life. If the news was full of stories of crime, I didn't watch. If I talked to people who were full of hate, I excused myself from the conversation. It wasn't long before my mood was easier to control as well as my thoughts. This process increased my standing as a newly released inmate from both prisons.

This is not to say that we won't be back in these people's life as some point, but we first need to get our foundation strong. Build our self-worth to a point whereas it cannot be easily shaken. Then these people we love and care about can be around, and perhaps we can even change their way of thinking and acting. We need to secure our footing in our own self-worth first. Then we can let our light shine onto others.

When I got out of the Michigan Department of Corrections, I went to visit my grandparents. My grandfather who I called Pop's, was two years into lung cancer and was bed ridden. He stayed in a hospital bed in the living room of my Grandparents house. Most of the time he was out of it and anything but lucid.

My mom would make little comments about how she lost all patience when I was born. I quickly realized that this was a potentially hazardous environment to my new mental freedom. Sadly, my Grandfather, (Pop's) lost his battle to cancer. His passing reaffirmed my dedication to my freedom and I purposely avoided my mom and her comments until I had my freedom foundation firmly established. I had to push off the negative as part of my training for freedom.

Likewise, one of my friends from the area wanted to hang out now that I was out and around. It didn't take long for me to realize that although years had passed, he hadn't changed mentally. He wanted to hang out and get wasted. That was his goal every weekend. Hang out and get wasted. Aside from wanting to get wasted I realized everything out of his mouth was negative, towards everyone he spoke about. I had to politely bow out. This was not a productive road I needed to be going down.

Escape Your Prisons

The training that took place is like maintenance on a vehicle. If you fail to get an oil change then eventually your car runs poorly if at all. I had to stand vigilant with the negative things in my life and constantly will them out. Whether it was people, thoughts, or things. In doing this, I was building a strong foundation for my self-esteem, and self-worth.

You would think that training comes before your escape and that is partially true. This is an ongoing process and as you face the new challenges you have, to prepare for them and constantly adapt to the new situations.

Athletes do not just train until they get in the game and stop training for future games. They continue training as the face new opponents all through out the season. Thus, we constantly train for our freedom. In this way we can maintain and not fall back into the convict role.

This is a battle not a game. We battling to keep our freedom and prosperity. We have more at stake than just a trophy. We have our freedom and happiness on the line, and that is worth more to me than any trophy. This is valuable enough to live and die for.

Chapter Overview:

- Training for escape is a continuous and ongoing process.

- As new challenges come at us, we must be dead set on not accepting anything doesn't coincide with our beliefs in ourselves.

- It is all about believing in our worth and preserving our freedom.

Chapter 5

When I was released from the Michigan Department of Corrections, I was told by my parole officer that that the recidivism rate for ex-convicts was just over 50 percent. Hat means that for one out of two inmates released from the penitentiary would end up locked back up. This is insane.

It makes me wonder how many people who have escaped their self-imposed prison, have fallen right back into the old ways and re-created their fences and walls. I feared this would happening to me. I set out to watch people and see how they handled and maintained their escapes.

When I talked to people in my life that I knew suffered from self-hate, they put on a brave face and claimed they never had an issue with this. I soon realized that they had never escaped. They were still living in the same world of self-hate and low self-esteem. They just got a lot better at hiding it from the public.

A girl I used to work with was the picture of happiness at work. She had an up-beat personality and always had a smile for anyone who entered the room. What the world didn't see was that she went home every night and ate her feelings. She hid behind a wall of low self-image and replaced self-esteem with food.

During a counseling session with her, it came out that in high school she was told by a popular boy in her school that she was fat and unattractive. She liked this boy and his opinion matter to her, so she took it to heart. Her walls and fences started going up at an alarming rate.

She craved acceptance that she didn't get at school or at home and it led to a deep depression. When her parents told her, "this depression she was in wasn't normal", she changed and put on a happy face to gain their acceptance. It was a mask she wore to gain her parents and everyone else's acceptance. She wasn't truly happy, and the low self-image issues were still there.

She dealt with it as an adult the only way she knew how. She ate, and as her weight went up, her esteem dropped lower and her prison fences grew higher. She didn't feel worthy of anyone's love or attention.

Escape Your Prisons

She has since been in one on one sessions with me and has followed the process that I used. I am proud to say that at last report she is happily married with a child on the way. Although she reports that its an ongoing process to maintain her freedom.

Maintaining is just that, an ongoing process. The battles do get easier with time, but the battles still come at you. One way I have found to maintain your own freedom and self-worth is to help others. Helping others to overcome their prisons keeps the process in the forefront of your mind and actually-helps you to maintain your freedom.

It doesn't take all that long and you start to realize that you're are becoming genuinely happy in life. I know, crazy right! I thought the same thing.

One day I was sitting at home after a long day at work. I was tired and sitting in the lazy boy and I was truly ok with my life. I had no regrets as to where I was in life and aside from some goal's I hadn't quite reached I was happy with life. This was a shock!

Happiness was a concept I had only dreamed about and never thought, it actually-exists. To me, it was like a fairy tale people talk about. Like Santa Claus or winning the Powerball. Something happy to think about. Not something that could be obtained, especially not for people like me. Yet, there I was, Happy!

Helping others not only kept the process in the forefront of my mind. It brought joy to my life. I found that I got joy and fulfillment from seeing other people overcome obstacles in their lives. This sharing soon became a drug for me. It is also one of the reasons I am writing this little book. Not for the money, because Lord knows I will probably spend more on editing and cover design then I will make selling copies. I legitimately get joy from helping others. I think you will also.

If you have gone through these pages and are battling through trying to escape your own prisons, follow the process I went through and I think you will be pleased at what you can accomplish! You are worthy of love, kindness, and respect. You can accomplish anything you choose. It will take work, and there will be obstacles to overcome. You can do it. Do not let anyone define who you are or where you can go.

You have the power to decide who you want to be in life. Past failures do not define you. Self-hate, poor self-image are things of the past. You are a great, and beautiful person who is wonderfully made. Create the new definition of who you are and break free of the prisons that have held you back from living the life you truly deserve to live!

Your freedom is at your fingertips, the prison walls are ready to have a hole knocked in them, the fences are right there ready to be scaled. A life of happiness is waiting for you on the other side. Now is the time, and today is the day. **Take your freedom!**

Conclusion

People live in self-imposed prisons due to negative life experiences. They become bound by a belief that they are less than equal to other people and unworthy of love, kindness, respect and prosperity. These prisons can affect financial and social experiences and lead to severe depression, unfulfillment, regret and suicide.

The good news is that it doesn't have to be this way. You can break free of your chains that bind and lead a life of happiness. The process I went through can help you live the life you were meant to live. You can have a great self-image and find the happiness and joy in life you were meant to have.

Through quiet truth/self-reflection, you will find what kind of prison you are in and how you got there. Once you acknowledge your prison you can develop a plan to escape. You will have to put in work and make a conscious effort to avoid the negatives that lead to those dark thoughts.

Replacing those dark self-hatred thoughts with positive ones will lead to a clearer mind. Focusing on the small positive victories in your life make it easier to push back the darkness and allow the person you were meant to be to shine through.

Maintaining your freedom is an ongoing process as you face new challenges. However, helping others break free of their prisons will keep the battle in the forefront of your mind and not allow the negatives in life to sneak up behind you and shank you in the back.

The battle is real for many people. It affects more people than you could imagine. If you are

Escape Your Prisons

someone who has been living in a self-imposed incarceration it is time for you to escape your prisons and get on a path from chains to happiness.

Escape Your Prisons

Contact Information

Interested in contacting Jody? Tell him about yourself, he loves hearing from people and sharing life experiences. You can contact Jody Via e-mail or by visiting his website listed below!

E-mail: Jforehand@escapeyourprisons.com

Visit my website:

https://www.escapeyourprisons.com/

Escape Your Prisons

About the Author

Jody Forehand is a former inmate of the Michigan Department of Corrections. He served fourteen years and ten months as an inmate. He served thirty-two years in a prison of self-loathing before he found the process that allowed him to escape.

Jody is currently a part-time motivational speaker and full-time Health Safety & Environmental Manager for an Oil field company in North Dakota where he has resided for the past decade.

Escape Your Prisons

Made in the USA
Columbia, SC
14 February 2020